SIDDHARTHA AND THE SWAN

Children and adults alike, we all love stories. When we share a story with children we can help them to explore important areas of human experience and encourage them in their spiritual and moral development. The Greek myths, stories from the Bible, and the countless tales of the world's many religions show that humanity has long used story to communicate its deepest values and codes of behaviour. The magical qualities of a story speak directly to our hearts and illustrate and share profound truths. Imaginatively entering another's world, we return with insights to apply to our own lives.

We have enjoyed writing and illustrating this story from the Buddhist tradition. We hope you and your children will enjoy it too.

Adiccabandhu & Padmasri

Published in association with
The Clear Vision Trust
by Windhorse Publications
11 Park Road
Birmingham B13 8AB

Text and illustrations
© Clear Vision Trust 1998
Design Dhammarati
Illustrations Adiccabandhu
Printed by Interprint Ltd,
Marsa, Malta

British Library Cataloguing in
Publication Data. A catalogue
record for this book is available
from the British Library
ISBN 1 899579 10 9

Adiccabandhu & Padmasri

SIDDHARTHA
AND THE SWAN

WINDHORSE PUBLICATIONS

Long ago in India, there once lived a king and queen.

One day, the queen had a baby boy.

They called their little baby Prince Siddhartha.

The king and queen were very happy.

They invited a wise old man to come and tell the baby's fortune.

"Please tell us," said the queen to the wise old man.

"What will our son become?"

"Your son is a special child," he said.

"He could become a great king one day."

"Hooray!" said the king. "He will be a king like me."

"But," said the wise old man, "when this baby grows up, he might leave the palace because he wants to help people."

"He'll do no such thing!" shouted the king, as he snatched the baby back. "He's going to be a king!"

Prince Siddhartha grew up in the palace.
All the time the king watched over him.
He made sure that his son had the best of everything.
He wanted Siddhartha to enjoy the life of a prince.
He wanted him to become a king.

When the Prince was seven years old his father sent for him.
"Siddhartha," he said, "One day you will be king, so now it is
time to begin your training. There are many skills you need to
learn. Here are the best teachers in the land. They will teach you
all you need to know."
"I'll do my best, father," replied the Prince.

Siddhartha began his lessons.

He did not learn to read and write.

Instead he learned how to ride a horse.

He learned how to use a bow and arrow, how to wrestle, and how to use a sword.

These were the skills that a brave king would need.

Siddhartha learned his lessons well. So did his cousin, Devadatta. The two boys were the same age.

All the time the king watched his son.

"How strong the prince is," he thought, "How clever.

How quickly he learns. What a great and famous king he will be!"

When his lessons were over Prince Siddhartha
liked to play in the palace gardens.
All sorts of animals lived there – squirrels,
rabbits, birds, and deer.
Siddhartha liked to watch them.
He could sit so still that they were not afraid to
come near him.

Siddhartha loved to play by the lake.
Every year, a pair of beautiful white swans
came to nest.
He watched them from behind the reeds.
He wanted to see how many eggs there were.
When the eggs hatched he visited every day.
He liked to watch the babies learn to swim.

One evening Siddhartha was by the lake.
Suddenly he heard a sound above him.
He looked up.
Three beautiful swans were flying overhead.
"More swans," thought Siddhartha,
"I hope they land on our lake."

But just at that moment one of the swans fell from the sky.
"Oh no!" cried Siddhartha, as he ran to where it lay.
"What's happened?"
"There's an arrow in your wing," he said.
"Someone has shot you."

Siddhartha spoke softly so that the swan wouldn't be afraid.
He began to stroke it gently.

Very gently, he removed the arrow.
Then he took off his shirt and wrapped it
carefully around the swan.
"You'll be all right now," he said.
"I'll look after you."

Just then, Devadatta his cousin ran up.
"That's my swan," he shouted.
"I shot it. Give it to me."
"It doesn't belong to you," said Siddhartha.
"It's a wild swan."
"I shot it, so it's mine." said Devadatta.
"Give it to me now."
"No," said Siddhartha.
"She is hurt and I want to help her."

The two boys began to argue.
"Stop," said Siddhartha. "In our kingdom if
people can't agree they ask the king to help.
Let's go and find him now."
The two boys set off to find the king.

When they got to the meeting hall everyone
was very busy.

"What are you two boys up to?" demanded
one of the ministers. "Can't you see how busy
we are? Go and play somewhere else!"

"We haven't come to play. We've come to ask
you to help us," said Siddhartha.

"Wait," called the king when he heard this.
"Don't send them away. It's right that they
should ask us."

He was pleased that Siddhartha knew what to
do.

"Let the boys tell their story," he said.

"We shall listen and give judgement."

First, Devadatta told his side of the story.
"I shot the swan. It belongs to me," he said.
The ministers nodded their heads.
That was the law of the kingdom.
An animal or bird belonged to the person
who shot it.
Then Siddhartha told his side of the story.
"The swan isn't dead," he argued.
"It's hurt but it is still alive."

The ministers were puzzled.
Who did the swan belong to?
"I think I can help," a voice said.
An old man was standing in the doorway.

"If this swan could talk," said the old man, "it would tell us that it wanted to fly and swim with the other wild swans. No one wants to feel pain or die. It is just the same for the swan. The swan should not go to the one who wants to kill it. It should go to the one who wants to help it."

All this time Devadatta stood silent.
He had never stopped to think that
animals had feelings too.
He felt sorry for hurting the swan.
"Devadatta, you can help me to look
after the swan if you like," said
Siddhartha.

26

Siddhartha cared for the swan until it was well again.
One day, when its wing was healed, he led it down to the lake.
"It's time for you to leave us," said Siddhartha.
Siddhartha and Devadatta watched as the swan swam out into
the deep water.

Just then they heard the sound of wings above them.
"Look," said Devadatta, "the others have come back for her."
The swan flew up into the air to join her friends.
Then they all flew over the lake one last time.
"They are saying thank you," said Siddhartha, as the swans flew
off towards the mountains in the north.

notes

About the story

This story of kindness and compassion comes from the Tibetan Buddhist tradition. It tells of the early life of the Buddha. He was born Siddhartha Gautama, son of a ruling member of a warrior clan in northern India. It is said he grew up in luxury, shielded from the unpleasant aspects of life. In his twenties he suddenly became aware of the suffering of old age, sickness, and death and, determined to discover the cause of this suffering, he abandoned his luxurious lifestyle for the life of a wandering holy man.

For years he wandered in the jungle, learning from teachers he met along the way. Finally, realizing that he was no nearer to an answer, he sat down to meditate under a peepul (bodhi) tree. It is said that sitting there, moving into deeper and subtler states of mind, he finally gained insight into the true nature of existence: he attained Enlightenment. He understood the cause of suffering and how to alleviate it. Thereafter known as the Buddha, or "One who is awake", he spent the remaining forty years of his life wandering the roads of India, teaching others how to gain Enlightenment for themselves.

Initially the Buddha's teachings were passed on orally; it was 500 years before they were eventually put into writing, at the beginning of the Common Era. Fuller, more poetic accounts of his life which began to emerge included many stories, such as this one, about the young Siddhartha. Buddhists today do not necessarily see these accounts as historically true, but as pointing to deeper truths about what it means to be a human being. The message of the story of Siddhartha and the Swan is of such significance that the story has now been adopted by many schools of Buddhism.

In retelling the story for children, we have combined the old fortune teller and the wise man who gave judgement on the swan into the same character. We have also attributed a change of heart to the Buddha's cousin Devadatta. While keeping to the spirit of the original story, we wanted to assert the possibility of change for the better and encourage children to develop empathy with other living beings.

Exploring the story

Adults can enhance the natural process of learning by encouraging children to talk about the story. Open-ended questions will encourage children to make an imaginative entry into the world of the story to empathize with the characters, and to make connections with their own lives.

Which part of the story did you like best, and why?

Which of the people in the story would you most/least like to be? Why?

Why do you think ...
- Siddhartha helped the swan?
- Devadatta changed his mind?

What do you think would have happened if ...
- Siddhartha hadn't found the swan?
- The wise man hadn't given his judgement?

Themes to develop

Kindness to animals
Talk about
- how we care for our pets
- how we can tell if they are ill or unhappy
- caring for wild animals in the environment

Settling arguments
Talk about
- how you feel when you fall out with someone
- how you settle arguments
- to whom you go for advice

Making amends
Talk about
- a time when you realized you had done something wrong
- how to put things right
- saying sorry

BUDDHISM is one of the fastest-growing spiritual traditions in the Western world. Throughout its 2,500-year history, it has always succeeded in adapting its mode of expression to suit whatever culture it has encountered.

WINDHORSE PUBLICATIONS aims to continue this tradition as Buddhism comes to the West. It publishes works by authors who not only understand the Buddhist tradition but are also familiar with Western culture and the Western mind. Parents and teachers will find a wealth of background information amongst these books.

Introductory Books

Suitable introductory books include **Introducing Buddhism** by Chris Pauling

Who is the Buddha? by Sangharakshita

What is the Dharma? *The Essential Teachings of the Buddha* by Sangharakshita

Change Your Mind *A Practical Guide to Buddhist Meditation* by Paramananda

These and many other titles are available from Windhorse Publications

Orders & catalogues

Windhorse Publications 11 Park Road, Birmingham, B13 8AB, UK Tel [+44] (0)121 449 9191

Windhorse Publications Inc 540 South 2nd West, Missoula, MT 59802, USA Tel [+1] 406 327 0034

Windhorse Books PO Box 574, Newtown, NSW 2042, Australia Tel [+61] (0)2 9519 8826

Clear Vision

The Clear Vision Trust is a Buddhist educational charity which promotes understanding of Buddhism through the visual media. Clear Vision's education team produces a range of resources, books, and videos to support high quality religious education and spiritual, moral, social, and cultural development. It also provides in-service training on Buddhism for classroom teachers.

Recommended videos include the award-winning **Buddhism for Key Stage Two** and **The Monkey King and Other Tales**

Clear Vision 16–20 Turner Street, Manchester M1 4DZ, UK Tel [+44] (0)161 839 9579

The FWBO

Windhorse Publications and Clear Vision are associated with the Friends of the Western Buddhist Order (FWBO). Through its sixty centres on five continents, members of the Western Buddhist Order offer meditation classes and other activities for the general public and for more experienced students. Centres also welcome school parties and teachers interested in Buddhism.

If you would like more information about the FWBO please contact **London Buddhist Centre** 51 Roman Road, London, E2 0HU, UK Tel [+44] (0)181 981 1225

Aryaloka Retreat Center Heartwood Circle, Newmarket, NH 03857, USA

In the same series

The Monkey King

A stirring jungle tale of greed, heroism, and mangoes. Beautifully illustrated, this delightful tale from the Buddhist tradition is retold in a style that will enchant the young reader.
Illustrated by Adiccabandhu

ISBN 1 899579 09 5
£5.99/$10.95

The Lion and the Jackal

A community of lions and jackals learns that friendship is built on trust and generosity. Beautifully illustrated, this heartening tale from the Buddhist tradition is retold in lively fashion to engage the young reader.
Illustrated by Adiccabandhu

ISBN 1 899579 13 3
£5.99/$10.95

About the authors

Adiccabandhu is an ordained Buddhist. An author and illustrator, he works for the Clear Vision Trust, a Buddhist educational charity. He has over twenty years experience in education as teacher, trainer, and producer of educational resources, and has four grown-up children of his own.

Padmasri is an ordained Buddhist who has enjoyed a long career in primary education, both as teacher and trainer. A mother with grown-up children of her own, she now directs Clear Vision's education work.